VILLA STELLAR

VILLA STELLAR

by
George Barker

FABER AND FABER
London & Boston

First published in 1978
by Faber and Faber Limited
3 Queen Square London WC1
Printed in Great Britain by
Western Printing Services Ltd, Bristol
All rights reserved

British Library Cataloguing in Publication Data

Barker, George, b.1913
  Villa Stellar.
  I. Title
  821'.9'12   PR6003.A68V/
  ISBN 0-571-11292-7

Dedicated to Hedley and Fiona Marten

Poem as Dedication Written at the Waterfall of Vyrnwy

What, my dear Hedley, are we doing here at
the source of water falling from so high that
it might have found its fount at clouds in which no
hand had a hand? And why with two
small children who do not so much ride on the shoulders
of stones as flitter round about the fallen boulders
not seeking, as we do, some sense of origins hidden here
but having found it? What is this sense of origins they have
      found
here among the cascading murmurations of that sound
you and I know the poem takes its fountaining inception
from? I think it possible that this perception
consists of the logos at the heart of all natural facts
as forgiveness crowns the fulfilment of all human acts
and as the pathway through the Commission-conifered forest
began among beds in which the newborn child first
saw its own death's-head on fire in the air. How
can I ask why you, Hedley, and I are here now
when all that I know is, simply, that we are
here seeking among the fallen gardens and water falling for
the knowledge of why we are here? We search among
the stones and whispering water and the reflections what long
we shall seek and not find, the impulse of
that recurring and continual suicide of love
like the small water that rides to the crest of the mountain
and casts itself over to create the poem and the fountain.

VILLA STELLAR

I

Why the white oxen? Simply because they are gone.
May they haunt the bright springs of Clitumnus for ever.
But I too have watched their delicate lolloping into
and out of those marzipan springs welling up like the
    melting of rainbows
among emerald meadows painted afresh every morning
and seen Renoir's blood drip from their horns in the
    evening
and known that I was not dreaming. Now they are really
    gone. Only
the proprietor's dog sleeps outside the café at noonday
and I speak in vain for the dead. The small temple so
    plainly
forgotten a mile further down the new highway
that in the rain a long distance lorry driver idly
supposes it nothing better than a derelict public lavatory,
there, there a dead friend and I sat sipping Frascati together
and watched the great white bullocks unwinding ribbons
of water like rainbows from around their ankles, and we
    know when we see
the funeral phantasmagoria of what will never return.
So may the great white oxhead that sleeps undisturbed by
    even
Propertius or the susurration of a hundred poplar trees in
    the evening
haunt these springs of Clitumnus for ever.

II

Was it the river of yesterday by which we were walking
when I heard its voice as by aural illusion murmur:
'Tomorrow you will not believe that today I spoke only to
      you
and to the one who walks invisibly beside you.
You will henceforth believe I have always existed; that
any old innocent strolling along these banks receives the
inexplicable consolations of water continually talking to
those who can hear it, always with one beside him
who cannot be seen, for this unforeseeable friend
is the person whom you were yesterday, who will neither
      remember
nor believe what it is that he cannot remember.
But I have not always existed, nor often spoken.
Only on this one day, this first person singing day,
I have discovered my source in your own overpowering
impulse and need simply to listen to me. And even
though you and I are equally ignorant of archaic Aramaic
we both know that the poem, like Venus, is born from the
      spume
of the stream as it leaps and speaks among rocks and stones
or as the haemal cataract of the heart cascades
down doubts and mires and old circumstantial disasters
whispering and whistling what we hear as the poem.'

III

And by that old road where I stood among the
umbrella pines and the disinfected vines and the fallen
masonry of an empire so bankrupt of human love
that it haunts us with precedents, there, as evening
stalked with its Roman lions along the balustraded sky
I heard the voice of a friend say: Forget me. Forget me.
O summer lakes among the evening mauve mountains of
little Iseo, with a white sail flickering among the
thunderheads and the lightning flashing in kisses, how
how can I never, never remember?

IV

As she stepped out of the train at Rome I saw that she wore
an old brown cloak that made her look like a female
    Franciscan
stepping into a comic opera to upset the principal soprano.
Kingsmill brandished a bottle of Martell. We got into a
    Mercedes.
We drove out to Albano. There in the evening cottage
set in the gardens of the Contessa's Victorian villa
we settled down to the brandy. The room filled with
    shadows.
We drank by the light of a fire. I saw two faces.
Kingsmill, who looked like a very wise small shepherd boy
and—but who ever heard of a bald-headed Fury?
That night finished up at eleven o'clock the next morning.

V

Why does the little rotunda temple on its hill by Albano
seem always about to be overwhelmed by enormous
storms of torn cloud as the sunlight turns its spreading
and radiant vans over that turbulent sky?
When I ascended the hill with a friend on a cold March
      evening
it seemed to us both as though we were walking up into
the last great staircase of space. But there it hung
just up above us, that sibylline little temple, like
a spiked crown of pillars, and through it Time and
constellations visible for no more than a moment
and the moon like a Maenad, turned in the cyclix agony of
revolving, evolving, revolving.
And, at the centre, only the temple stood still.

VI

There may, of course, be some point in the usage of
        language
as though it was written not by a man but a rather
sensitive machine. But are we to deduce from this that
the writer is not a person but an instrument constructed
like a typewriter capable of working by itself in a corner?
'Look! No hands!' And am I at all concerned with
the judgements passed upon itself by such a gadget?
(I recall a Remington that refused to write 'Herman
Melville': it insisted that the correct rendering
ran: 'Merman Melville'.) And I do not speak of
the ego but of the conscience. Given the
terrible choice I would rather listen to the lies of
the Flatulent Ass than the truths of the Tenor Computer.
For the Tenor sings, as we know, truths without serious
        intentions.
My Flatulent Ass brays lies to make you love me.

VII

Not in the poet is the poem or
even the poetry. It is hiding behind
a broken wall or a geranium
or walking around pretending to be blind
seeking a home that it cannot find.

Into the ego that has emptied out
everything except its abstract being
and left only a shell, the poem then
moves silently, foreseeing
its purpose is to haunt the shell like singing.

VIII

Who are you and why are you here? You are the ones whom
I always found standing there at the first assignation
and therefore are here and always. I mean those allegorical
instances that vault like acrobats into the ring of our lives.
Tony, leaning at that half-open french window with
the rain descending on Italy outside, his easel
lashed to his shoulders with a coil of rope like
an acolyte carrying his own crucifixion,
lifts a hand and is gone. And the hand leaves me
all love written on the air. And you, chantress to seals,
coiled there in a wicker chair with your eyes wandering
among the invisible peaks and lakes not yet created,
you speak to me of the love I still seek to understand.

IX

When the typewriter is suffocated with roses and the villa
    window
so shuttered with the coloured lantern slides of sunset that
    I sit
in a room full of shadows on fire, noiselessly lurid
like the flames of those who wish they were damned, when
    the mirror
over the mantelpiece catches the first livid gleam
of the cut-glass moon as she enters, the dying Diana,
when the wine bottle shines with its mirage of instant
    solutions
beside the bed of those who wish they were dead,
when outside the window the wolf lowers its muzzle
onto its paws, and sighs,
then for a moment if no one is there I believe that
I can believe in the possibility of human communication:
that, if one closed one's eyes and opened the
prongs of the forked tongue, if one saw the head of the
    Medusa
framed in the mirror there on the mantelpiece,
and one said: 'Regardez la lune,' if only, perhaps, then,
    some day
one might find it possible to speak to a second
person who, unlike a friend, cannot forgive one.
Who cannot forgive one simply because one cannot
forgive the second person because he is also us.

X

When was that morning when
the heart leaped out of my
breast and turned handsprings round
the shuttered bedroom? What is
the current price of love?
The price of love is a cup
of spiked belladonna or
a kick in the ballocks and
a jack-knife stuck up under
the fifth forgiving rib. Such
a price is exacted not
by any abstraction but
by a physical law
pronouncing the victory of
arbitrary instruments: the
coil, the Dutch cap and
old Colonel Condom or
the Great Liberty Pill.
When I draw the dawn
sheet down from your sleeping
face to reveal the dreams
that tend you in your sleep
I see that their arms are full
of love-lies-bleeding.

XI

Yes, that corner fireplace in the cottage by Lake Nemi
how it flickers its flames among my then and now to
illuminate these images like trophies. I see the arbutus
bough hung like a pair of bronze antlers over the mantel-
    piece
catching occasional and fiery gleams out of shadows and
for an instant transfiguring a broken branch into
the Golden Bough of Diana. And why not, since with my
own hand I broke that branch off the tree that time had
    elected
to plant where she once slept at her altar and
where the murderer could never sleep? Why is
that wood sacred? It is sacred because, if you walk there
you will perceive that this wood and the handmirror lake
happen to be haunted by a presence of human dereliction
that walks there as though we might be gods again.

XII

And if I had only watched the mists of that morning a little
      longer
I, too, Kingsmill, might have seen the sun emerge and then
disperse them. But I watched you, my friend, and not them.
I saw you surrender to the contemplation of those opalescent
mysteries the David star of your mind
as you stood by a Roman aqueduct. You watched your
      painting happen
as the mists obscured your vision and were in turn
bedizened and gilded by it. When the speculative
imagination walks among uncertainties the
shapes and configurations of its strangest interpretations
seem to be seeking to find it. What, Kingsmill, did you see
in those morning presences that rose slowly from the lake?
These are the clouds that the god of the machine descends
      in.
You, too, saw that the sun also rises, the vapours fade and
      disperse,
(You, too, saw Hesper bathe her face in the morning)
if only we stand and wait by the lake a little longer.

XIII

And there in the May Borghese Gardens with a foam of
blossoming flowers around us we sat at a small table
she with a hat like a huge waterlily and a glass of iced
lemonade sweating in sunshine and the Roman sky like the
interior of an enormous pearl, and semi-precious lizards
    scooting
among the hibiscus. I said: 'It is pleasant here.'
She answered: 'The sun is not Scottish. I feel faint.
Yes, it is heavenly here. But I think of the misted November
evenings and clouds coming up over the Cairngorms
and the violent gusts of rain and the cold amber streams
    jumping
among the lichened gullies and the rowan hissing in rain
and a single horned sheep standing still as stone against
    the sky.'

XIV

That Austrian beerhouse in the street of the Obscure
      Bottle, how
often I sat there downing my eleventh pint, hypnotised
by the Lowenbrau blue lion rampant and watched the door
for that convivial friend to enter who of course did not
even exist then, let alone choose to join me as
I learned how jaded the company of a besotted boor
particularly when he is me. One should not encourage one's
self to despise the first person singular too much or
one may find that the frog of the alter ego has
inflated its little self with the hot air of congratulation
to the point of double explosion. But this particular evening
I was not alone: a presentiment sat opposite me,
her painted black eyes wide open, long legs crossed, and her
silence answering the questions I could not ask, such as
'What chariot brought you here?' or, 'Do you disappear if
I call for another beer?' And then I knew that
I had invented you out of the moral zero of
my self-swallowing snake. You were actually there.

XV

Have those who have been there ever returned again from
the bed of the Circean bitch or the baths of sea-green Venus
or those pools where white oxen emerge dripping rainbows
    from the
coloured springs of Clitumnus, have they ever returned
    again
without in a sense having died? What have they left
    behind them
caught in a twisted vine by the path up the hill to Albano
like a scrap of old newspaper? It is nothing less than the
perception of forfeited paradise, which, once we have left it,
once we have lost it, looks like dirty old newsprint. I have
left in cloudy Umbrian mountains the knowledge that
what we once found is the vision that we lost
only because we found it. There are some things that enter
the ceremonies of everyday existence only
when they have been exiled for ever, such as innocence
foregone or the inexpiable fact that what we have done
cannot be undone, not even by the gods, or the actual
palace we turned away from, when, set among our illusions,
we believed it to be a mirage. This is the lost love.
Thus the purpose of the lilies of Solomon as they loll
about in the derelict gardens is to remind us that
we have forfeited them simply because we
collected too many and anyhow they are not ours.

XVI

But is there, is there a face that I shall meet somewhere
and recognise that I have reached the twin lakes of a vision
not to be seen elsewhere, the sibylline cave of words
and echoes no other oracle can ever evoke: it is the poem.
Will that face speak to me of those Cumaean interpretations
I have not dreamed could ever seem to seem to be?
If I ask: what is the poem? Will that face turn
the prisms of its vision upon me like an arithmetic
proving it also exists? And prove that its purpose
is also possible? O marvellous face of images and
caves that I cannot find, of mirages that mirror faces
I could believe that I shall meet somewhere,
are you the true hallucination that declares to us once and
    for all:
'There are no illusions'?

XVII

So the Contessa invited us to attend a piano recital
in the music room at the villa. Kingsmill refused and
Elizabeth Roberta Cameron put on her Wellington boots,
masked her enormous eyes in goggles of mascara and
we traipsed rather moodily up the garden path to
sprinkling Chopin. A bald young German maestro
milked the Steinway, and the Cameron sat nibbling at
a large bowl of macaroons. I observed that she had
removed one of her Wellingtons and surreptitiously
scratched away at her instep as with her other hand she
fished for more biscuits. She leaned over and whispered:
'Very soon you will have to excuse me. I am
utterly tone deaf to all instruments except the bagpipes.'
We got up and left. She sneaked a few macaroons
as she rose from her chair. The young German pianist
played us back down the garden path with another exquisite
    Prelude.

XVIII

Where are you, hours of my hope that sprang like dancers
whirling in circles it seemed must be everlasting?
What was the name of that brilliant ballet you conducted
there in the Italian theatre of a time so long ago
that, to me now, it seems like a midsummer
dream performed in a sunlit garden at midday. Who
has dismissed those dancers, where are they flaunting now,
the blonde tresses tossing and the flying feet and the
    ribbons
writing desire on the air, and lyrical waterfalls rising
among the cardboard rocks? Who was it disbanded
your dervishing circles and cut the cord of the curtain?
What I know, now, but did not know then
is that the dance that begins of a midsummer midday
always invokes the rain. The manager whose dancers
abandon him abandon him for one reason
and one reason only: he does not deserve them.

XIX

That sparkling and white morning of the bay at Lerici
with slopping waves rocking the harboured boats when the
    wind challenged the
snorting sea-horses and fought with the palm-trees—it was
    all enamelled and
gilded and whitewashed and together we strolled in its
    hyaline
like two figures stepping into an animated Impressionist
    painting.
On the seafront old gentlemen in dashing trilbies and white
    silk neckerchiefs
pretended to be Max Beerbohms. Operatic young fishermen
    stood about
waiting to burst into arias. The sun polished the water
as though it was christening it. There must have been
    hibiscus.
And I saw all this reflected in your morning eye
still cloudy, like Rubens, with dreams of the dying semen.

XX

When she is old
and nodding by the fire
better memories than those of my verses will keep her
from the cold.

XXI

The telephone rang and a voice said: 'It's Henrietta.'
I responded as decently as considering the hour I could.
She said: 'Come and admire the sunrise.' I went and
    admired it.
The doves twittered in their cages outside the villa
    window and
'Do you observe', she continued, 'how the arbutus and laurel
down there in the garden entwine together as though to
asphyxiate one another? I am, my dear, seventy-eight
    years old
but it still moves me near tears to look down on those two
    trees.
For once, long ago, in Ancona, I stood beside a laurel
and thought I would die of love.'

XXII

Can the heart ever return to the house of its origin where
a window looked out onto that prospect of fields and
    flowers, always
it seemed patterned in the harlequin tints of
early childhood? And where a conjuring stream trans-
formed a dead dog into Hermes with wings and stars?
What was it this little river said
to the child as he sat staring into its transformations?
'You cannot catch the fish,' it said, 'they are too quick.
You cannot catch them. They are too small for the hook.
Why not a net?' But the child sat there, watching
the harlequin hours flickering and glittering
as they poised in the eddies or shot into caves or weeds.
Had he been asked: 'What is the river saying?'
this child would have answered: 'Nothing. It cannot speak.'
Can the heart ever return to the house of its origin, or
has Hermes gone?

XXIII

The Contessa sat by the window fingering the black notes
    of the piano.
I saw the sunset begin to fight its way over the
    Mediterranean
in a noiseless allegory of the futility of speech
and indeed of everything save the cloudy mutations we
    think we believe in:
those cloudy mutations in which all aspirations and all
    dreams
and all human determinations, as the sun falls,
fade into the supercession of night and stars. Are they,
    these cloudy presences
the hereafter of yesterday's equally futile illusions,
the hallucinations of which there is no original
excepting that first dream of an ejection from a garden
where we once walked without knowledge?
The Contessa rose and led me out into the arbour
where we sat without speech, looking at the sky.

XXIV

To divine the spring that is hidden among heartbroken
    stones we
do not set to with sledge-hammers or the latest thing in
pneumatic road drills but we sit by the gutter and listen to
the verses of underground water that seek to speak to us.
If we hear the invisible vocables as they voice their
almost ineffable need to be known, to be comprehended,
we converse with dead kings and kingdoms of an eternology
which winds cannot abrade or the deposits of industry
    denigrate
or the lord of the machines tear to pieces until it surrenders
the dragon's tooth. The broken idols of Shelley still
stand like skeletons in deserts, denoting those hidden
springs where we hear history whisper among the silences:
'But speak the word only.' And as we approach those
    springs
knowing there are no gods in this wilderness we
watch with incredulous eyes the lilies of Solomon
rise and twist up from fissures, and the word
divest itself, dancing, of seven veils. They are the voices
of what can never be heard until the human
spirit has broken, and found that the underground founts of
its lachrymae weep with words. And what we hear
is the conversation of Memnon. And shall these bones speak
concerning a geology constructed entirely
out of dead truth and ossified ideals? What they say
wordlessly in the underground galleries of the
past is, simply: 'We are buried but we are not dead. Let
the dead bury the dead if the dead are dead.'
And when I lean down and listen I hear the clepsydra of
    history
not like a clock of tears but like rainbowing rain.

XXV

She walks with me beside the lake.
  It is about seven o'clock
of a spring evening. The sky
  is overcast and sometimes the
mist turns into rain. The surface of
  Nemi is heavy and sad and
offers to us no reflections
  as we walk in silence. And high
on its rock the grey monochrome
  town hangs down crags like collapsing
rubbish dumps. Some lights flick on in
  the mist and if we halt we hear
the spitting of rain on large leaves.
  There are various kinds of spring
flowers about in the copses
  —bluebells, violets, but now on
this melancholy evening
  they look like badly painted daubs
by a sick child, and as we walk
  the moon emerges silently
from out of a cloud and slowly
  whitewashes a domed chapel
and hanging houses and broken
  wall of the water-colour town.
We walk in a silence like mist
  and knowing that there is nothing
at all to say we listen to
  an absence which does not speak to us:
'You know perfectly well there is
  nothing that anyone can say.'

XXVI

But is there a story to tell? There is always a story
of people who seek among streets and the dead ends of the
  mind
for what they have lost
as they looked for the house and the homeward angel.
What are you doing here among the wrack and ruin of a
hope that the hope still mourns for? Each of us lives
in a mansion constructed of mirrors that reflect only
the emptiness of all rooms save the chamber of wax
effigies who died for us. What I wrong when
I write these lines is condolence to these dead
who do not know they are dead and therefore continue
to sit around in the catacombs of my days and drink coffee
as though death was life, which, for all I know,
it may well be. Then Adam may rhapsodise in the
mouth of the worm and the sleepers make love in the grave
and I meet again as I enter
the lily-wreathed bedroom
an I who sits there believing he is still breathing.

XXVII

If we could truly tell
what impulses of the heart
pull that knot apart
would it be just as well?
I see you where you lie
on a bed by a wall
like any Lorelei
naked and mythical,
but I also saw
that Aphrodite wakes
fatal Eros for
all our sleeping sakes.

Out of the seeming
Atlantis of our dreaming
where even the dead and
gone sleep on the sand
I watched you rise up for
all the world like a sea-
breathing anemone or
my own Anadyomene
born beyond the shore
of what is possible. We
who have drawn Eros out
of unknown seas, we know
better than to doubt
that such things can be so.

I looked into my heart
and found, sleeping there
in its most haunted part,
Eros with your wild hair
rise from those shadows. Then

I looked in my heart again
and saw it was Primavera
stepping out of your mirror
and those old frozen seas
flashing between us
a bridal bed to please
even sensual Venus.

I have held her small
conched shell in my hand
and heard in it the choral
of the foam born and
the sirens and the fishes
as they mate and cling
on bridal beds of coral:
'In the kingdom of wishes',
I have heard them sing,
'everything comes true.'
All that I wish today
is tangible in you.

XXVIII

There was this cage of wild doves hung at the wall of the
    villa
among occasionally flickering vine-leaves and shadows that
    never
seemed, somehow, to move with the sun, for all things were
    so still in
that sunlit garden that sometimes I thought it existed
in a trance of ideal abstraction. The dull hum of the housefly
hung in the air by a vine-leaf seemed like the far off
    functioning
of those heavenly engines we think, sometimes, we overhear.

What did those doves dissemble that I do not know?
O wilder symbols of a devotion that is never free,
you spoke, dusty tongues, of a love that is happy in chains
simply because the purpose of this love is to enter
the glasshouse of what it loves. This incarceration
works in its own reverse, for that cage is the heart of a dove
seeking in turn servitude in what it loves.

XXIX

Do not look at me. Do not look. You might see
past and through the person pretending to be me,
and at the far side of that spiritual illusion
only an obscene machine of sexual passion.
If you extend a hand to me it will reach
nothing at all until the fingertip touch
sets a nerve jumping and the clockwork prick
triggering up. I beg you—for your sake—
do not look at me. I have never existed.
There never was a person standing where I
deluded those whom I love a person stood.
Only the obscene machine has persisted
jerking and jockeying and not knowing why
I have never existed. Nor should.

XXX

Let us acknowledge, then, that the mindless pigeons of
    Skinner
demonstrate that the doves of the spirit happen to be a
    delusion:
the sleight of hand this involves is elementary.
All doves that behave like pigeons exist: they are pigeons.
Doves that behave like doves do not exist because all
doves, even those of the spirit, behave like pigeons. Thus
there are not doves. Why does the human psyche decline to
render itself susceptible to my analysis?
There can, of course, be only one rational explanation:
if the soul declines to enter the intellectual laboratory of
my curiosity, then it is, quite demonstrably, not there.
What enters this laboratory exists. There are no doves
in my laboratory. Therefore there are no doves.

I do not permit pigeons to enter my Orphic dovecotes.

XXXI

Hung high on a side of that lovely valley by Albano
that opens itself like arms down to the sea
we found, as do only those who deserve it, the little
    restaurant
called, as it should be, Il Paradiso. Set on a ledge
in an arbour of vines and mimosa it overlooked farms and
woods and the tilted fields that lessened and faded
till they reached the rim of the dazzling Tyrrhenian as
green as old glass. Why does that lovely valley
as now in my mind's eye seem always full of pale pink and
yellowing flowers? There we would sit and watch
the afternoon sunlight perform its ballet of waltzing
slowly along the horizon, and through its evening
    declensions
make our way back to the villa. Somnambulants
of a dream that ceased only when we slept, we seemed
    fatally
drawn in a trance towards that small death from which two
always rise up like swansongs.

XXXII

'And as for this little matter of human love,' said the
    Contessa,
'I once preferred money. Now I am not quite so sure.
The older I get the more vulnerable I find myself
to the fascinations of the rather improbable, such as love.
"What is love," said the poet, and informed us, "It is not
    hereafter."
Love is the fact of its object. Without it nothing can enter
the sanctum sanctorum of our subjective perceptions
like the hole in the dome of the Pantheon for the god to
    descend through.
This is the here and the now. O the unforgettable brevity
of the lifetime of love that we perceive was love
only now it is gone. Everything expires as we turn the
deathray of our desire upon it. It is gone.
In this sense everything was, and never is. Look,
as I speak it is gone. Only the need persists and
jogs on through the appalling optimism of the possible
towards visions of love that like faces reflected in
passing trains disappear on the instant, simply because they
were in fact seen. If we had not looked, they might not
even have been there. Love,' said the Contessa, 'is what
    we do.'

XXXIII

There is of course nothing to say and no way to say it
that does not demean the essential verity of
all that lies sleeping at the heart of the matter.
That heart is perfectly conscious that its subconscious
    dreams are
falsified spoken of. Why should I not think that the
twenty-six characters are like a row of mynah birds
whistling in the dark about things which neither
alpha nor beta nor mynah bird can be expected
to know that they do not know? What is the language of
the heart that has turned to a grave-stone or the mind
that sits in a furnished room with its throat cut or
the spirit inured from birth to solitary confinement in
the cell that speech cannot reach or even our loneliness
    penetrate?
When the dolphin of the North and the dolphin of the South
meet in the seas of paradise, what if they call to each other:
'O brother! We still cannot speak!'

XXXIV

I write these autobiographical verses backwards, like
   looking down the wrong end of a telescope.
Why? Because then I see, diminished in the distance,
the once prodigious Wingless Victory
   still a tiny hope.

XXXV

How can we elucidate the laws of coincidence save by
assuming that time itself sometimes employs metaphor
in its purpose of illuminating what we would otherwise
    imagine
a matter of no importance? And furthermore what of those
unknowable dualities about which, in our knowledge, we
perceive only the half that happens to enter our perceptions?
I am trying to speak of the laws that govern the ceremonies
of our need. Why are the ones who will offer us
a bed or a bottle of brandy or the rope that may save us
always there when we do not want them but come empty-
    handed
when all that we need is a bed or a brandy? It is
because these unpredictable nurses know the right time to
    be there
but we do not. The coincidence of love operates
solely to serve its own purpose, which is to show us that
only it knows the right time. We do not know what we need
as those who offer it know that we need only
what we are offered and when we are offered it.

XXXVI

This is the true coincidence of love, that it occurs
only when it creates itself at the metaphorical moment
of its own purpose, and this purpose is
simply to happen, simply to prove it is needed, like
the Infanta Isabella's comment on Columbus:
'If those islands had not existed, they would
have risen out of the sea to crown his passion.'
I walk in parallel with you
blindfold down all these corridors and
save in the unlikely event, the somnambulistic coincidence,
    that
we remove our blindfolds at exactly the same moment,
we cannot speak of love.

XXXVII

What I see when I look into my memory to write this
    word is
the naked May morning tossing out her yellow hair by the
    little
watercress stream that sidles under apple trees. Her, too, I
have held in my arms and felt the butterflies flittering in
the heartbeat of her hours and heard her amorous syllables
uttering nonsense in the dawn chorus of birds. I, too,
have seen the May morning step out of her sleep by a tree
unspangling and shaking the daisy chains out of her hair as
she awakened beside me, and the uncurling fern trembled at
her dayspring matrix. Early in the white beds of dawn
I, too, have spread, like a fan, the knees of May.

XXXVIII

One day, perhaps, the sun will shine without shadows and
I shall see them for what they are, the bony caryatids
that stand between us and the sun, like those elephantine
    aqueducts
of Lazio seen in the sunset. What on earth are they holding
up on their granite shoulders, these colossi, these Atlases
of our moral imagination? Are they the principles
by which we agree to be judged, such as those that
the cut stone bleeds in the Decalogue or the pelican
declares as it tears at its breast or the tree instructing us
year by year in the victories of simple persistence?
These are the wholly artificial systems we have constructed
in order to protect ourselves from what appals us. They are
    the
shadows cast by a sun so marvellous that it would certainly
    blind us
without their supervention. Thus the moral systems function
like St Paul's dark glasses, to prevent our being blinded.

XXXIX

(a)

You ask me where I am going? Well,
I'm either passing through Italy on my way to Hell,
or, to put the matter a bit too wittily,
passing through Hell on my way to Italy.

(b)

This business of Greek poets meeting violent ends
such as being torn apart by wild dogs or women
or having eagles drop tortoises on their bald heads—
well, a commonplace life deserves a death as common.

XL

Will you say that it cannot be said? I know that it cannot.
But just as the child looks up at the face of its mother
or she down into those eyes that do not need to open
and in both hearts like a suffusion it arises,
like a suffusion of roses it exudes its
inexpressible existence, the love that works in silence.
I remember old Johnson: 'If Mr A has
experienced the inexpressible, then Mr A ought
not to try and express it.' But, Doctor, if we
did only what we ought to do, how bored the archangels
as they sit sharpening their pencils on the benches of
      judgement!
For sometimes it seems as though speech has evolved
      simply
to degrade what it seeks to describe, or to defile
what it seeks to define. Then I can see the ideos in the logos
stuck like the face of a clock on the shoulders of an ape
who cannot tell the time, but knows that it is spring.
We have yet to invent the words with which to speak of
      this love.

XLI

The Contessa sat in her chair and spoke to me not briefly
    of life.
'It is always over,' she said. 'Every commonplace moment
    commemorates
all that has been and gone like a single stitch holding
    together
the seamless shirt in which we burn at this moment.
But the marvellous dragons and symbolic kingdoms and
    hieroglyphs
depicting the life of the soul so invested, these
once living mythologies, these shadowing moralities, they
seem to live on in the flames of the shift on fire
like unkillable salamanders. This is the "meaning" of life,
the mythological moralities that insist on being seen
like those wars that evolve in clouds, or that odd love
which arises from the purely fortuitous meeting of sublunar
    bodies
sleeping in space, or those solar mazes constructing
the heart of the rose. All these allegorical appearances
walk out into the world of the everyday garbed in the
    gorgeous
robes of those principles that have evolved as aspirations
and heavenly dreams of a slug that crawled up out of mud.'

'My dear Contessa,' I replied, 'shall we take coffee?'

XLII

Elizabeth Roberta Cameron lay on the unmade bed
and the afternoon sun dazzled pinpoints through the
    Venetian blind
and the hour of siesta in suspended animation
held Italy as in a glass bowl of bedroom silence.
I could have believed that I heard the umbrella pines
    breathing
as they dozed outside in the garden, or that the sirens
lazing in the shallow waves that expired on the sands of
    Anzio
sighed in the murmur of the water, and that Lake Nemi
had one looked would have been seen brimming with old
    dreams
of Diana, the Murderer King, and that Oxford scholar
who stopped one night near Albano and found a book
gleaming and prophesying from a golden bough.
Elizabeth Roberta Cameron lies on the unmade bed
with one sandal on and the other in her lifted hand
and why give to verses this hour that belongs to Venus?

XLIII

There by that coral shore leans over
   the palm-tree to the sea
and there the crosswinged pelicans hover
   and crash into the sea,
there the huge hibiscus flower
   and flame beside the sea,
there the Aztec sun, sinking lower,
   hisses into the sea,
and there two absences walk on
   beside the bleeding sea.

XLIV

To all appearances the life serene:
tea in the afternoon with two old ladies; talk
of this and that, and who and who have been
seen arm in arm on a Sunday walk;
how well the new tomato plant; what who said
when the old cow died; why the milk was sour.
He sat and chatted with them by the hour
until the time came to go in to bed.

The floorboards of the ballroom open up.
The flames. The pillar of. Who are you. Blood.
Something is burning somewhere. Waltz of Death.
The fire. I am I am. The flesh. The cup.
He would start screaming if he only could.
I feel the fangs and smell the stinking breath.

XLV

That Norman tower crowns a crag on the seacoast of
    Apulia
among marble mountains that collapse into a peacock-
    flaunting sea.
Derelict and gutted and as gaunt as a great monolith
it caps its rocky stalagmite and dominates my memory.
Thousands of feet below four fishing boats on the green
    wave
lift all together in a dance. Old newspaper and orange peel
and dogshit on the mouldy floor. A plank of board across
    a slot
in a seawind wall. A poster stuck under the Norman
    dogtooth. And
like a huge disc on either side
the Adriatic far below extending to the rim of time
a kaleidoscope in which this tower flickers for an instant
    and is gone.

What is that glass that supervenes between all
we see and the I that sees it? So that we can never
so much as say: 'That is the truly unvitiated
and perfect Tree of Itself I observe here in
the gardens of verity, yes, that is the tree of the tree
and it never before was seen for what it is.'
The name of that observatory from which one looks out
    upon all things
is the First Person Obscura and always the rain
or tears of its imperfections supervene
and occlude the vision or mutilate the veronica.
But have we suffered enough today to empty the lachrymal
systems of our response? The 'I' of the conditional observer
like a machine of glass manufactures inexhaustible
supplies of that crocodile fluid, but only the innocent
weep tears of such clarity that, if we could catch one
and gaze upon all things through it, we might well see
that Islington High Street runs straight through the Earthly
    Paradise.

XLVII

Hand of my hand, rest.
Heart of my heart, sleep.
Bright eye of childhood count
the lambs and not the sheep:
may the shepherd keep
a watch over your bed
till every lamb and you
rest a dreaming head.

The monsters of the day
have fled to other fields,
and now the mothering one
her milk of moonlight yields
and the great hunter wields
his wonders in the sky:
may all the monsters of
night and the nightmare fly.

From the foal and from
the kitten, child and kid
as they dream within
the eye and shuttered lid
our shoddy world is hid:
may a Mary of dreams
show them it is not
as monstrous as it seems.

XLVIII

If my images seem a bit dusty it is merely because the
mirrors get cloudy the more we breathe upon them:
this shows us, at least, we still live. The image of doom
is the one and only image we cannot blur with our
     breathing.
Death stands with a matchstick stuck in his teeth
     muttering:
Man, you're my pigeon. And the undying demigods and
the industrious idols and the gorgeous goddesses
glance with a wink at the man with a matchstick who
     whispers:
Keep the last dance for me. And in the ballroom
the band strikes up to open the Rignarök.

XLIX

'But what I want,' said the Contessa, 'is a word like a
perfectly commonplace rose. I am sick of the bouquets
of broken mirrors and barbed wire and rubber bladders
    containing
specimens of someone else's intellectual urine
mitigated, if one is lucky, by only the faintest odour
of a self abjuring its pity. I am quite sick of
the honesty that insists upon gurgitating into my lap
simply because I am sitting here. I am also
profoundly mistrustful of an amoral despair so
always accessible that, like a phone by a bedside,
it accrues a debt it does not propose to pay.
This debt is the price of that self-indulgence enjoyed by
those for whom their despair is like financing an opera
to be performed in the privacy of the boudoir or
as I say, a telephone line directly connected to the
tomb of the absconded god. My dear, write me a word or
two like a perfectly commonplace rose, for
in the course of a long life I have not yet encountered
a rose that could whimper.'

L

Lunar alanna, lunar alanna,
the little white dove lies dead at the door
and no wind, no, no wind can lift the cold feathers
or brighten the dayspring eye any more.

And then the rain that falls out of the evening
and the new moon, like a white knife
transfix the heart, and, for an instant,
galvanise it into posthumous life.

LI

When you departed, Kingsmill, why did you leave your
humiliation behind like Van Gogh's ear on my kitchen table?
Was it to teach me again that the victim is always
the real victor, and that the prize cup contains a
simply delicious poison? This poison is the knowledge that
in love as in war we are all defeated anyhow, because
to win and to love is to die on the vertical points of
life as death. The opening of the first door
always, my dear Tony, closes the second for ever.

LII

Now this bloody war is over
no more soldiering for me.
I can hear the angel in the kitchen
washing up the crockery for tea,
and down the lane the donkeys and the children
splashing through the puddle by the tree
and the daffodils that should have died in April
ostentatiously continuing to be,
so now this bloody war is over
no more soldiering for me.

Us dead are up and dancing in the garden,
us dead are throwing parties every night
and the destiny of man is with the children
daubing every bleeding elephant dead white
and us dead men and the children in the garden
are dancing hand in hand such a helluva saraband
that the Church and State in bed think it's thunder
        overhead
as the children and us dead dance through the night.

LIII

How can I find a place in my heart to hide from
my own self in, and where save here in the heart can I find
    it?
Can you hide in mine? You cannot. There is no room in
that butcher's cave save for the one who hangs there
in a lifelong suicide. Come, lift the leaves. When you enter
what you see will disgust you. You will recoil
at the smell of the rotten meat and blanch at
so many bones. Those who enter the polyphemus
heart are always horrified when they find that
one-eyed gigantic ego squatting there like an
unkillable shepherd. There in the heart he
sits over a fire that died long ago, and I, Ulysses,
I hang here like a side of raw beef in my own rib-cage.

LIV

Neither Time nor the image of doom can disfigure them,
the gilded effigies who sleep in forgotten cathedrals or
sunk in dead seas of memories like pillars of salt
suffering no sea change. Invisible birds revisit their
seaweed-invested and wave-rocking sepulchres as
sometimes my recollections unveil those tidal
isles where they lie, and, for an hour,
their talking bones walk with me on the shore.
I, too, lying here in the sea-green dream, hear those
Shakespearian wings revisit me, the haunters of dereliction,
the seagulling screamers that waken me into a deeper
sleep that is populated only by apparitions.
And the golden sea polyps of rot sidle out of their eye-
    sockets
as those drowned effigies smile and die and the waving algae
lifts its veils to reveal that nothing is left of our love.

LV

But, tell me, are the formalities
of verse intended to constrain the
free wheeling imagination or
liberate it
as the mathematics of internal
combustion engines function so that
a construction of gas and metal
begins to breathe
in obedience to laws of which
it knows absolutely nothing what-
soever? Is the poetic impulse
an intellectual
necessity to control or to
liberate the imagination?
Well, let me remind myself that we
'make' love with a couple of rather
simple gadgets from which emerges
Aphrodite.

LVI

Always it evades me as I stretch out my hand.
Time and the wind erase the codex in the sand.
The towers collapse. The tombs continue to stand.

Kingdoms break up but nothing falls from the sky.
The murderer's dead but the victims continue to die.
Who hears four horsemen as the fifth rides by?

Snow is descending in the living-room. The
Golden Fleece is weeping in its tree.
Where are the angels that I cannot see?

A dead mouse stirs in the Great Pyramid.
Who is that fool asleep on the fiery grid?
Will no one tell the donkey what it did?

LVII

You want the moon? That is what you will have.
Her stalking insomniac down the staircase of night
haunting the bed, the cradle and the grave
like a psychotic sleepwalking parasite
gathering old rags and bones in a dirty cave,
you really believe she has got second sight?
Teach this hysterical lunatic to behave.
You want the moon? That's what you will have.

The water that you drink and bread you break
will fill your mouth with dust and ashes and
you will sup sorrow for a fishwife's sake,
the ego flower up like an ampersand
out of your ventriloquist head and make
moonshine of what you think that you understand,
and in your bed hideous Selene fake
a love for you as false as quicksand.

She will lie there in illusions of seeming
intellectual grace, delusions around her
feeding her with liqueur chocolates as she lies scheming
among the phoney lovers who surround her.
You want the Muse? When she starts screaming
like sirens inside your head and you have found her,
you'll lie there in her coiled verbs of dreaming
ejaculating black blood all around her.

LVIII

The children are gone. The holiday is over.
Outside it is Fall. Inside it is so
quiet that the silence seems inclined to
talk to itself. They will not recover
the summer of seventy-seven again, even
though they become, in turn, their own children.

I sit in my sixty odd years and wonder
how often before in this old house a man has
sat thinking of what is now, and what was.
But can it serve a serious purpose to ponder
upon the imponderable? There, there beyond a
fall glimmers the long-lost garden.

That garden where we, too, as in a spell
stared eye into dazed eye and did not see
that suddenly the holy day was over,
the flashing lifeguard, the worm in the tree,
the glittering of the bright sword as it fell,
and the gate closing for all time to be.